THE GREENPRINT

JORDYN BARBER

For my children

As I write this, another upgrade to the iPhone has just been released. I want it because it's better than the one I have now. It's designed to be.

Makes me wonder...

Why hasn't life gotten an upgrade? Life as I live it could use one— an upgrade to ease the stress of not having enough money to live how I want. Money is what it all boils down to for most of us. But what if that changed?

For those in the top bracket of the pay scale, let's be honest. You could use an upgrade too. Feeling disconnected much? Trying to stuff your soul with stuff? Reached the top and still feeling unfulfilled?

We can give ourselves something greater. A deeper, more meaningful experience that we can savor to our last moments and pass on to our children.

In these pages, you will find a design for a new way of life that optimizes ease, connection, and fulfillment.

Welcome to The Greenprint.

INTRODUCING *THE NEIGHBORHOOD*

The Neighborhood is a connected self-sustained high-tech residential and commercial community designed to boost ease in life. The bulk of what The Neighborhood consumes is made in The Neighborhood by the people who live there, the residents. All residents have access to The Neighborhood's amenities in exchange for a 20-hour workweek.

A definite change from our current system in which you work for money to pay for your needs. In The Neighborhood, you give your 20 hours and you receive a home, quality healthcare, fresh food, dedicated schools, entertainment, and money. We all love money. Together we can get more of it.

The Neighborhood creates abundance. An abundance of food that residents cannot eat on their own. An abundance of creative products that residents cannot use on their own. The excess is sold to people outside of The Neighborhood. The profit from what The Neighborhood sells is then split equally amongst residents as all residents are equal shareholders in The Neighborhood. The money received can be spent however they want. Since residents have no costs in The Neighborhood, it is easy to build wealth.

This redesign of the economy fosters a connection between residents. Developing deep connections working together adds more meaning to our lives, eases the disconnected empty feeling we share, and boosts our quality of life. Knowing the person who is growing your food, teaching your child, and building your home increases your quality of life because everyone is held to a higher standard in transparent connection.

This superb quality becomes our brand. Helping us to sell our products, produce, media, vacations, and special experiences. The more we sell the more money we all make. Yet the bottom line never supersedes the quality of our product, the wellbeing of our residents, or the land we live on.

The Neighborhood is an upgrade that will slow the stress vortex we spin on now. This book details broad strokes of the vision of The Neighborhood with the intention of creating future editions, growing a loyal base, and making The Neighborhood a reality. Take a journey into the future and enjoy your trip.

PART I

FUELING THE NEIGHBORHOOD

A full stomach, stable economy, and powered technology fuels stability

A FULL STOMACH

Agriculture is the foundation of The Neighborhood. How we approach agriculture is of the utmost importance because it feeds all other aspects of our life. The goal is to produce food, fabric, building materials, fuel, and medicine using innovative techniques that boost efficiency, productivity, and abundance without sacrificing integrity.

Our neighborhood uses a plethora of techniques to produce fresh food that we can enjoy and export. As a hub of ingenuity, the farming grounds include a mixture of indoor climate-controlled structures, outdoor pastures grazed holistically, forestry fused in permaculture, and integrated gardens throughout the community.

Leafy greens, strawberries, and fish.
An indoor aquaponic system produces leafy vegetables, select fruit, and fresh fish for our consumption. The aquaponic system fuses aquaculture (fish farming) with the hydroponic technique to grow produce without the use of chemicals. The fish create fertilizer for the plants, which in turn clean the water for the fish, creating a closed-loop cycle that is sustainable and easy to maintain.

Meat, potatoes, and shirts.
Our agriculture falls in line with restorative practices, strengthening the cycle of the ecosystem by replenishing the earth we take from. Using polycultured no-till techniques, we grow a variety of produce without wasting space, using pesticides, or exploiting the soil.

Growing cotton alongside alfalfa keeps Lygus pests from destroying the cotton crop without pesticides. Rotating cotton with sugarcane and/or wheat replenishes the soil and manages pests naturally. Replenishing the soil and maintaining a lively ecosystem must be key in our treatment of the land and our animals. Maintenance of outdoor pastures is done using holistic management which keeps the soil rich while providing the cattle, sheep, and goats the food, exercise, and freedom they need to live comfortable lives. Our animals are treated with the utmost respect as we know happy animals create feel-good products.

Almonds, lumber, and bees.
Agroforestry and beekeeping combined gives us double the product on both ends. A large forest farm produces nuts, fruits, medicine, fabric, and building materials while supporting a healthy environment for bees to give us honey and wax. Our philosophy is to integrate and diversify wherever possible, creating the most efficient and abundant process.

Flowers, pears, and your personal choice.
Along with the acres of land dedicated strictly to the main farm, there are edible gardens throughout The Neighborhood. Imagine sitting on a bench, reading a book, and eating a fresh apple picked from the tree you catch shade under. Every home is fitted with a personal garden. Residents can opt into a gardening service where a professional gardener tends to your garden every week so you can enjoy the benefits of fresh food or beautiful flowers in your home without worrying about maintenance.

FARM TO TABLE

We have grown accustomed to the ease of eating and we should embrace convenience while offering experiences to further connect.

Restaurants
From fine dining to dive bars, our neighborhood has eateries from all genres of cuisine using our local resources to create delightful food that we can enjoy and bond over. Types of restaurants in The Neighborhood include fine dining, family table, diner, sushi bar, and rotational styles.

Grocery stores
One large main store provides everything we offer packaged and on display as any grocery would. Smaller markets in the pockets of residential boroughs offer convenience for residents who need a quick grab of items without having to go to the center of town.

Food stands
Pop-up street food gives us the straightforward food we know and enjoy along with experimental cutting edge foods that our neighborhood chefs want to introduce.

Dining hall
Food court-style venue that doubles as a community space. There is a main community dining hall and a dining hall for the school.

Delivery
Online delivery service from all restaurants, food vendors, and grocery stores is available.

$$$

All of these eating experiences are available to non-resident customers for a price. Residents and customers receive the same quality product. Customers can buy our food onsite and online.

STABLE ECONOMY

Redesigning how we connect economically means shifting our mindset from scarcity to abundance by managing our resources, reprioritizing our values from profit first to people first, and creating an environment for creative jobs.

SHIFTING TO ABUNDANCE

We live in an abundant world, yet we manage our resources terribly. In the USA, we have 3.5 million people without homes and 18.9 million homes without residents. Worldwide, 815 million people live without enough food to lead healthy lives, yet we waste 1.4 billion tons of food—enough to feed 2 billion people. We don't have a scarcity issue; we have a resource management issue.

Resource management is key in creating lasting economic stability. It tells us how much of what we have, how much we as residents consume, how much excess we have to sell, and how much we waste. Resource management does not limit what we consume as residents. Instead, it watches and predicts what we will need in the future, communicates with the departments that produce that need, and ensures we have enough of what we need. Resource management is an overarching department with several sub-departments of people and technology that help us track our inventory, predict trends of consumption, and boost productivity for export.

Every product is tagged with a chip that communicates with different devices. The chip goes where a normal barcode is now. Say we follow a package of strawberries. The moment the package is made it is barcoded with a chip. The first piece of data we receive is that the package exists which-added to all the other packages of strawberries-tells us how many packages we have created. When the package is sent to the store, the chip is scanned to tell us the strawberries are at the store. When a resident takes the package of strawberries, the chip tells us it's been consumed by a resident as opposed to paid for. Resource management keeps specific tabs on crops, products, homes, energy, resident skills, work hours, healthcare appointments, and anything else we produce or use.

PEOPLE OVER PROFIT

Our economy thrives because of a strong connected foundation. All of us working together in The Neighborhood to create quality lifestyles for each other creates a stable base and an incredible abundance of quality products that people outside of The Neighborhood pay good money to receive. The quality of our product is top-notch because it is a product that we consume. We are the front-line consumer of our product so inherently we will want it to be healthy, durable, and efficient. This close connection with pure product undoubtedly makes it competitive in the world market without having to sacrifice our well-being. No one in The Neighborhood is overworked, put into dangerous environments, or stressed over the fear of losing a standard quality of life. We trust that taking care of ourselves and our community first is the best way to create quality products that inevitably create abundant profit.

CREAM. That abundant profit is split in a very specific way. Profit is divided amongst the residents, initial investors, and The

Neighborhood bank. Initial investors get 5% of profit, The Neighborhood bank takes 15%, and the resident pool is 80% which is then split equally for each individual and directly deposited into the individual resident accounts. The Neighborhood bank accrues value for community projects, emergencies, and further residential aid.

The 20-hour workweek. We deserve to feel secure and not feel like at any moment the rug could be pulled out from under us. The direct trade of work for a quality life and ownership of that life frees us from the money chase for survival. Our continued goal is to lessen the number of work hours. Less work yet more efficient, focused, innovative work because we let technology do the tedious work for us. Less mandatory work hours leaves plenty of time to pursue personal passions. Family. Candy Crush. Making more money. It is important to note that any money made by residents inside and outside of The Neighborhood belongs to those residents. If you decide to move out, you take your money with you.

CREATIVE CONNECTED JOBS

As technology takes over monotonous jobs that are ripe for automation, we must focus on what we as humans do best—create and connect. Creation and connection are values pushed to the forefront computers and robots take over manual labor and tedious tasks. Although there is emerging AI that can learn, create, and connect, I believe that humans will always have a deep want to connect and create with other humans. It is not the tools we procure but the values we possess that will determine our fate as a collective species.

Creativity. In any field, creativity is used to solve problems, boost efficiency, and build innovations. In The Neighborhood, this principle applies to all fields, but let's focus on how it works for teachers specifically. Teachers use creativity to create a curriculum that engages and educates students. They are not asked to monotonously teach the same curriculum year after year. They are pushed to adapt, elevate, and evolve education with creative innovations. In a neighborhood like ours, teachers can work closely with engineers to build new technology that increases student learning.

Connection. Teachers working with engineers is the type of elevated connection our neighborhood produces. There is a specific department that solely focuses on making these connections happen. They are called connectors. If anyone in The Neighborhood needs someone from a different field to help them, they can reach out to the connectors who will facilitate that connection. Connectors also help identify inefficiencies in The Neighborhood that can be solved by better connections and then facilitate making those connections happen. Connectors work closely with psychologists and therapists ensuring that teams collaborate in healthy, productive ways. If any drama gets in the way of healthy production, connectors are the front-line alert. They can then send the team to counseling to work out whatever personal issues may be going on.

POWERED TECHNOLOGY

Using clean, renewable, and sustainable energy sources produced in-house, we create our power for the technology that eases our day-to-day life.

The Neighborhood uses an assortment of energy sources including solar, wind, hydropower, corn, and sugarcane.

Solar. Every home is self-sustained with solar power. A large solar farm offers energy to communal buildings.

Wind. Rows of windmills on the outskirts of The Neighborhood provide additional energy.

Hydropower. A running river circles around The Neighborhood, its movement yet another source of energy.

Corn and sugarcane. The farm grows both crops for food and energy sources. Corn and sugar are both processed for ethanol which can be used as an alternative to gas although all public transportation in The Neighborhood runs on electricity. Ethanol is also used in hospitality, medical, and manufacturing settings.

COMPUTERS, ROBOTS, AND SMART CARS

The Neighborhood works with technology to make life easier and more efficient for residents. Not only do we integrate technology in ways that improve our lives, we continuously innovate in the quest for efficiency.

Transportation. Smart cars, buses, and trains foot the bill for safe long-distance travel around The Neighborhood. Streets are hardwired with sensors that keep residents safe and vehicles aware of any dangers. The center of The Neighborhood, the town square, is a no-vehicle zone that opens up the space to foster community and more meaningful connections with fellow residents.

Computers and Software. Our neighborhood produces its computers and computer software in conjunction with having access to the brands we love and enjoy. We develop software that aids us in work, education, entertainment, and research.

Communication. We own our own fiber optic internet connection and develop our smartphones and communication app that is exclusive to The Neighborhood. The communication app, called I See You, allows a secure way to interact with the community, keep up to date on community news, and even aids in voting on particular decisions.

Resource Management. Specific technology sensors, trackers, and software are developed for the sake of resource management. This technology informs us of what we have, the trends of consumption, and how fast we produce.

Robotics. Our robotics division constantly churns out robots that help with manual labor in manufacturing, hospitality, and agriculture.

PART II

NURTURING THE NEIGHBORHOOD

A warm home, commitment to learning, and dedication to health create a comforting base from which we can grow

A WARM HOME

A space to call your own is the truest comfort of existence. In The Neighborhood, you have a variety of housing options customized to your lifestyle, equipped with the luxuries of modern life, and suited to stand on its own.

VARIETY

The Neighborhood consists of different boroughs each designed for specific lifestyles. Each borough will have its park, market store, and eatery so there's no need to go too far to get what you want.

Town. The town has condos clustered near the center of The Neighborhood where the action goes down. Close to the shops, restaurants, and recreational activities, living in town is for those who like to stay in the mix. Catered to the single crowd, most condos only have one to two bedrooms yet still incorporate an outdoor feature.

The Middle. An ever-changing borough catered to singles, newlyweds, and emerging families gives residents more space to stretch out and more room to build. The middle consists of multi-level single homes that can be easily expanded as the family grows. Great for singles who enjoy a bit more solitude and newlyweds who are planning to expand their family soon.

Settle Down. The settle down caters to emerging and established families. One-story sprawled out homes with the opportunity to add bedrooms along with large backyards perfect for young children.

Empty Nest. A borough dedicated to an older crowd. A mix of recent empty-nesters, grandparents, singles, and couples. The most traditional-styled homes are positioned in a way that gives ultimate privacy yet the safety of a nearby neighbor.

Resort. The last borough is the resort. Built to cater to people outside of The Neighborhood but also used as staycations for residents. The resort is a villa with separate suites, a world-class spa, a fine dining restaurant, and a large pool. The reason the resort is important is it further strengthens The Neighborhood's ability to entertain guests and make money while also giving residents a space designated for relaxation in the event they need to cool down from any stressful situation. The Neighborhood is not a utopia. There will be conflict as humans naturally fall into drama. The resort is one of several tools in conflict cool down.

STAND-ALONE LUXURY

Every home is equipped with the standard luxuries of modern living and boasts enough space to fulfill the resident and their family. Every home has a kitchen, dining space, living room, office, master bedroom, family bedrooms, guest bedroom, bathrooms, garden, laundry room, and storage.

Rooms are completely furnished. Every kitchen comes with appliances already installed. A smart refrigerator that can tell you when it's time to get new milk. An electric stove, dishwasher, and garbage compactor. Living rooms are furnished with a large TV, bookshelf, and couch. The laundry room includes a washer and dryer. Bedrooms, office spaces, and bathrooms all include proper furnishing.

The homes are fully furnished, yet customizable. A resident interior designer can be brought in to help any resident who wants to customize their space. Interior designers capture your style and work with resident artists and furniture makers to create unique pieces that fit you. Residents are always welcome to bring or buy furniture they like from the outside and can ask for any of The Neighborhood furniture pieces to be moved out of their homes. The only requirement is that appliances must be compatible with the self-sustainable flow of the house.

Ideally, every home can stand on its own. Creating its power with solar panels and recycling a set amount of water. Yet every home is connected to a backup power and water source that can kick in if the power runs out.

COMMITMENT TO LEARNING

"If all you had was academic ability, you wouldn't have been able to get out of bed this morning. In fact, there wouldn't have been a bed to get out of. No one could have made one. You could have written about the possibility of one, but not have constructed it."

Sir Ken Robinson

Education in The Neighborhood is designed to create competent, empathetic, and creative residents. Pyramid to sphere. Education keeps the sphere power structure intact by ensuring everyone has the knowledge needed to run every aspect of life, leaving no one person or group with exclusive access to knowledge or skill of any kind. A growth mindset teaches us that all minds can learn all skills and our children embody that to the fullest, knowing how to operate in all facets of The Neighborhood and therefore, the world. There are six different schools in The Neighborhood, each catered to a specific phase in life.

EARLY EDUCATION

The Neighborhood's early education schools focus on cultivating a love of learning by creating a safe loving space, encouraging adventure, and teaching with playful action. Early education consists of three schools: the nursery, toddlerhood, and preschool.

The Nursery (Birth to Walking)

The nursery is available for all parents who need a place for their baby to be during work, a night out, or a mental break from the stress of parenthood.

The nursery specializes in baby care. Caregivers make sure babies are fed, entertained, comforted, and clean. Babies are fed according to their parents' wishes. They keep formula in stock as well as accommodate breastfeeding mothers. Baby food and fresh healthy whole food is kept on deck for feeding.

Caregivers engage babies in play personally and with the aid of technology. Music is interwoven in the environment to build skill and promote a creative connection to sound.

Babies have a set school schedule like the rest of the schools, but their schedule coincides with parents' work schedules.

Cameras in the nursery capture every moment of the baby's care to ensure transparency and security. A live stream is always available to parents via the I See You app. Plus parents can access past footage and view it as well.

The nursery offers support beyond caring for babies and includes caring for new parents. New parents can reach out for extra help if they feel overwhelmed. The nursery connects them to a therapist who can help ease the transition.

Toddlerhood (Walking to 3)

Once a baby begins walking they are moved to Toddlerhood. This school is safely padded for toddler action. The environment is set for them to explore on their own, always under a team of teachers' observation, with different sections offering experiences that push specific skills.

Music section includes toddler-sized instruments as well as recording stations that allow them to record themselves and hear it back.

Playground section where toddlers can run and play on low indoor and outdoor play equipment.

The arts *and craft section* includes painting, clay modeling, sand, and water play. *Building section* includes jumbo LEGO bricks they can use to build houses they can play in and furniture they can sit on.

Technology section features pre-reader coding activities. *Imagination section* includes a variety of experiences including dress-up, toy kitchen, hospital, grocery, and more settings to enhance creative play.

Self-care section has accessible potties, sinks, mirrors, and their locker for personal items.

It is not entirely free time. Group activities led by trained instructors include sports, swim lessons, musical instruments, foreign language, and writing. Guided sing-alongs reinforce empathy, emotion management, and common knowledge.

Preschool (3 to 4)

At the age of three, children are ready to advance to preschool. The preschool is set up similarly to toddlerhood as in there are sections of the school devoted to different skill-building. Preschool introduces more structure into the child's learning. Some tasks must be completed before the school day is over, teaching responsibility and accountability. This is also when the teachers begin to take note of the best learning times for each student. This follows them throughout their educational experience as schedules are tailored to their best learning times. Students also work with each other to create projects. Projects may include putting on a play, cooking a three-course meal, or building a chair. Every skill learned has a product created by the student. This product is uploaded to their file where they and their family can always view what they've created over the years.

PRIMARY EDUCATION

The goal for primary education is to lay a solid foundation of mastered skills and knowledge that ensures our students are ready for their immersion into the work done in the community and therefore the world.

Grade School (5-9)

Students study specifics on how everything in The Neighborhood works. They visit parts of The Neighborhood and become interconnected experts.

Students learn not only how to work in existing systems, but to also build and create their own. They are encouraged to constantly innovate. Communication, creativity, maintaining healthy relationships, conflict resolution, logic, emotional management, problem-solving, grit, and self-motivation are all skills instilled in the students to ensure they can thrive in any setting.

Like in preschool, the students' schedules vary depending on what time suits them best — morning, afternoon, or evening. Group classes are kept to small sizes and each child receives individualized attention.

The primary school is a leap in size as each class has its own space. Classrooms are designed to evolve and implement real-world learning. For example, the farming class has an indoor farm connected to an outside garden. These simulated spaces ensure students in their age range have a safe, easily guided space in which to learn real-world skills. Once they've mastered growing beans outside in the dirt and a hydroponic system, they have a foundation to stand on when they work the farm in intermediate school. Every key function of The Neighborhood has a classroom that emulates it.

Parent participation is key, but the school does it all regardless. Since we want to keep parents involved and updated on the status of their children's learning, every parent is given one work hour every two months to spend in teacher conferences and various workshops for parents. There is no homework outside of school.

Intermediate (10-12)

The intermediate school is quite small because students spend most of their learning on site. Students are assigned a neighborhood department that rotates every month. It is designed to introduce students to every aspect of The Neighborhood so they can make an informed choice on what they want to develop their true trade-in.

The school does have classrooms in which students come to reflect on their experiences, review past knowledge, and take safety seminars or protocols for the department they will join for the month.

They help to build homes, tend the farm, assist in the hospital, teach younger children, clean neighborhood buildings, code neighborhood apps, customer service for online buyers, and a myriad of other actions that keep The Neighborhood running.

Along with neighborhood assessment, students pick hobbies and activities they are interested in further mastering. Sports teams, music, art, filmmaking, science, architecture, business, debate, and a variety of clubs are integrated into their education. They are always supported in their passion and pushed to learn it all.

After Intermediate, students will have a deep understanding of The Neighborhood as a whole and will be ready to go even deeper into the department or departments of their choosing.

HIGHER EDUCATION

Trade school (13-16)

In trade school, students choose exactly what department they want to work in and begin interning. In this way, students obtain real experience in that field working their way up. Students can choose to go into one trade or even choose up to four. They can transfer at any time or commit to one. They decide where to go depending on their interest, demand, and referrals from professionals they came into contact with during intermediate.

It is important to note that trade school for some professions are more rigorous than others. For example, if a student wants to become a doctor, the student cannot commit to any other trade program because of its rigorous schedule.

Resident students are funneled through this school and move into placement by 16 years old.

Placement(16-18)

After finishing trade school, students are placed in long-term professional positions. Their placement depends on their interests, recommendations, and resource management. Students may be placed in more than one position. Placement for students begins at 16 where the student is now receiving their percentage of profit from The Neighborhood. 50% of the students' profit is locked into an account they access when they are 18. In the meantime, they receive financial counseling to prepare them in case they do choose to leave The Neighborhood upon turning 18. If they choose to stay, they continue in their perspective placements unless they desire to transfer.

Embarkment

Students who do not wish to stay in the community have the option to embark. Anyone turning 18 years of age who chooses to leave will take self-sufficiency tailored to their future goals. Each student who embarks creates a plan for themselves and receives a mentor to help them achieve their goals. Students may plan to travel the world, attend college, start a business, or jump into any creative options they want to explore.

Embarking students can take all funds received from their placement along with any money their parents choose to give them. Students can also apply for assistance from The Neighborhood bank if need be. Embarking students always have a place to come home to if they choose.

CONTINUED LEARNING

Skill Transfer

If any resident begins to dislike their position, they can join the skill transfer program. Skill transfer works a lot like trade school being that residents learn on the job. If the job they currently have is becoming more efficient and needing less labor, residents are encouraged to participate in skill transfer. Resource management triggers if skill transfer is needed. Skill transfer hours count as work hours.

Survival Standard

Every year, residents take part in survival standards. The course lasts for four hours and is counted as work hours. In the course, residents are prepped on what to do in case of any emergency. Residents learn skills needed in case all technology fails.

Library

The library is a dedicated space for hard copy and digital books alike. It is open to all residents for free and to non-residents for a fee. The library hosts events for The Neighborhood. It is a beautiful quiet place where learning and discovery flourish.

Research

Every department has a research team that monitors and discovers what is working, what is not working, the effects on The Neighborhood, and the potential of possibility. Their work keeps us in tune with integrity and sharp with innovation.

$$$

Our school track is open to a select number of non-resident customers for tuition that rivals competitive private school prices. Students receive the same quality education as resident students and have the option of joining The Neighborhood upon placement. Non-resident students have access to school meals, clothes, and transportation from their homes to The Neighborhood which is all included in the tuition.

DEDICATION TO HEALTH

"The current belief is that medicine is to be valued for its use during illness. But this point of view has to change. It must be to see that one does not fall ill."

Sri Sathya Sai Baba, 1980

The Neighborhood is designed to ensure healthy and easy living. Stress is the number one contributor to disease. The Neighborhood is designed to take the stress out of life for its residents. Less working hours. A home without the worry of rent. Easy access to fresh, organic, locally grown produce. This innovative lifestyle alone boosts health. To further support and sustain our collective health, our team of dedicated residential health care professionals works in a redesigned healthcare system that is comprehensive, preventative, immediate, and loving.

COMPREHENSIVE

Our healthcare is a marriage of western and holistic methods. The technical term for this marriage is integrative medicine. It operates on the foundation of treating the mind, body, and spirit with techniques from both systems that have been proven effective, yet always choosing the least invasive solution first and trusting the body's innate resiliency.

Mind, Body, Spirit

Our hub of healthcare is the wellness center. A fully operating hospital that provides all the services a high-end comprehensive western hospital boasts. Surgery, labor and delivery, labs for blood work, X-rays, pediatrics, emergency care, etc. It also provides holistic services such as acupuncture, massage therapy, aromatherapy, nutritionist, meditation, yoga, etc. The wellness center houses mental health and relationship therapy. Dentistry offices are located in the wellness center as well. We ensure all of our health services are in close proximity to promote communication between all departments communicate to better help patients.

In addition, the wellness center houses a cutting-edge pharmacy where chemists and botanists work together to craft innovative and conventional medicines. An on-site indoor farm cultivated just for pharmaceutical uses, along with an equipped lab allows for chemists and botanists to merge their knowledge and work together in a way that benefits us all.

PREVENTATIVE

Every year, people die from preventable diseases. Heart disease, cancer, strokes, and chronic lower respiratory disease take many lives before they are ripe of age. Many of these illnesses can be remedied by consuming a healthier diet, being more active, receiving therapy, having healthy relationships, and cutting out destructive behaviors. But in our current way of life, it is hard to make healthy decisions. After a long day at work ensuring the rent or mortgage is paid, it is easier to grab a fast food option and spend the rest of the night sitting in front of the television.

Wellness Coach

Every resident is assigned their own wellness coach who checks in to make sure residents feel supported in their health journey. Wellness coaches are the frontline of preventative care in The Neighborhood. They check-in and observe if a resident may be stressed, depressed, or tired. If a resident is stressed out from being a new parent, the wellness coach arranges remedies such as reaching out to childcare, providing the parent some alone time, and setting the parent up with a mental therapist. If a newlywed couple who is leaving the honeymoon phase is depressed and has yet to reach out for therapy, the wellness coach can spot this and set them up with a relationship counselor. A wellness coach spots general differences in health and sets up a plan for the resident right away. It is important to note that any resident can opt-out of having a wellness coach and/or following a plan set in place by their wellness coach.

Checkups

Along with the wellness coach, residents are urged to visit their general doctor, psychologist, and dentist for two in-depth checkups a year.

IMMEDIATE

Accidents happen. The Neighborhood is prepared for any incident inflicting a resident. Fast-paced transportation, a plan for having all hands on deck, and faculties ready for emergencies ensure better chances of healing from an unexpected injury.

Emergency Care

Our facility and team are prepared to deal with any life-threatening emergency quickly and carefully. There is a plan amongst the healthcare team to be enacted in case of emergencies. Any patient in critical condition is always treated with priority. Residents rest easy knowing that if an accident occurs help is a minute away.

Resource Management

Outside of life-threatening emergencies, residents need to be able to make appointments and get seen quickly when they are not feeling well. Resource management ensures that there is always time available for patients who need urgent care. They also work with all departments of the wellness center to ensure efficiency without sacrificing integrity.

LOVING

All of our health care professionals handle patients with empathy, patience, and care. It is the goal of our health care team to infuse love into every patient's experience. Love is not all sunshine and rainbows. It is reflection, truth, understanding, support, and growth. We understand how important it is to have honest supportive relationships with those closest to you and, most importantly, yourself. In a country where drug abuse and suicide are the top contributors to lower life expectancy, The Neighborhood tackles disconnection by connecting people to the passion and love that life has to offer.

Healthy Relationships and Self Love

Mental health is of the utmost importance in The Neighborhood. There is no such thing as utopia or heaven on earth because the human condition always squeezes in a tinge of drama. We expect no difference in The Neighborhood and want to be prepared to handle inevitable emotional and relationship conflicts. Couples going through a divorce in The Neighborhood always have access to supportive therapy. Any person having a falling out with family or friends will have access to on-demand counseling.

Along with two mental checkups, a year, and the support of the wellness coach, people who are feeling down and disconnected are always able to come in and reach help at any hour. A plan is put in place to create a supportive group of friends and get the resident involved in something that brings out their innate passion. Our top priorities are self-love and making sure patients take control of their happiness.

Our therapists do not string patients along to keep their pockets full and rent paid. Instead, they pack punches in their sessions by listening and giving the patients their ultimate true reflection along with a plan of action to help them achieve better lives.

$$\$\$\$$$

Any service our healthcare department offers is available to non-resident customers for a price. Customers can become members of our healthcare plan to receive wellness coaching and ensure they have access to all amenities year-round. Resource management calculates how many outside members we can accommodate and never prioritizes profit over quality. Residents and paying customers alike receive the same quality healthcare service.

PART III

FULFILLING THE NEIGHBORHOOD

Being heard, feeling safe, and having fun

BEING HEARD

Everyone in The Neighborhood has a voice that is valued. The Neighborhood uses a secure in-house app for residents to discover friendships, share creativity, and make decisions about how The Neighborhood runs.

I See You

Our resident-only social media app is called I See You or ISY for short. ISY makes it easy for residents to connect and receive the latest news of The Neighborhood. Event invites, creative works, and new ideas can be shared via the app.

Voting also takes place via the app. When a new policy is introduced for The Neighborhood, it has to receive a popular vote to be enacted. In addition to voting, residents can propose or challenge policies via ISY as well. Residents vote for a variety of entertainment purposes such as the theme of a festival or a revamp of The Neighborhood logo.

Town Hall

Instead of a board or city council, the group of people who are responsible for the ease with which The Neighborhood runs are the heads of departments. Similar to how a big-budget film is made, heads of departments are in constant contact to ensure The Neighborhood's success and continue to innovate the future.

The Neighborhood is a complete democracy that runs within the confines of a founding set of guidelines. Town Hall provides a physical space where everyone is heard. Residents share approval or disdain for aspects of The Neighborhood and the heads of departments are present to take notes and feedback. A sync feature in ISY offers instant visual polls of how residents feel about particular aspects of The Neighborhood. At the Town Hall meetings, the financials are presented to residents along with an overall summary of business progress.

1 800 PR

Any resident who needs help getting their creative works seen, meeting new friends, or finding romantic interests can seek help from a resident-centered PR agent. PR helps the resident connect with healthy, honest, and transformative tactics.

Being Remembered

Historians keep The Neighborhood's journey documented via photos, films, and a written record.

The Neighborhood has a cemetery on-site which is linked to a digital database where people can read about deceased residents and see any photos or videos of their departed.

FEELING SAFE

A secure neighborhood is essential for the well-being of the residents. Our security team operates on the foundation of transparency, prevention, intervention, and empathy.

Transparency

Truth is in transparency. Fraud and violence alike are less likely to happen when it is easy to be seen. Lying is decimated in presence of truth. This is why surveillance is key. All public spaces of The Neighborhood are captured by cameras.

There is no behind the scenes secrecy in The Neighborhood. Every resident has access to company financial records and can visit the spaces where products are processed. Not only is The Neighborhood transparent amongst residents, it is transparent with the world.

We create transparent media to share with the world. From documentaries on our farming techniques to live streams of our town halls, the world can take a peek at our way of life and feel like family.

Prevention

Entry Checks. Residents and non-residents alike are scanned for weapons upon entry into The Neighborhood. Non-residents are prohibited from carrying any type of weapon into The Neighborhood. Residents reserve their second amendment right to bear arms, but their weapons must be fingerprint protected.

Collective Mental Health. Residential mental checkups and observations of wellness coaches are essential to ensure residents are not looking to hurt themselves or others. The Neighborhood works to support people in times of anguish to prevent any acts of violence from occurring.

Diplomacy. Trained professional resident diplomats travel on our behalf to create healthy relationships with neighboring communities, states, and countries. We intend to sell products and experiences worldwide. With that intention comes the responsibility to have open and effective communication with local and global communities.

Lawyers. A team of resident lawyers ensures we are abiding by state and federal law. They work with every department head, especially the finance head. Lawyers ensure our taxes are paid, our buildings are up to code, and our processes are in line with the law.

Engineers of Defense. Resident engineers create technology that protects our neighborhood in case of an attack whether it be man-made or a natural disaster. These technologies are inherently nonviolent and solely focus on defending The Neighborhood in case of an attack, storm, earthquake, etc.

Intervention

911. Any resident or non-resident can call neighborhood security in case of an emergency. Security arrives swiftly and is ready to handle any emergency.

Non-violence Commitment. Our security team is dedicated to nonviolent measures even when faced with violent offenders. Equipped with defensive tools and tactics our security can capture offenders without taking their lives.

Empathy

Our Own Protection. To be clear, we only use our security to police our neighborhood. Outside police are not welcome to patrol our community. If local or federal agents are looking to come into our neighborhood they are greeted by diplomatic security detail and lawyers to discuss what their intentions are.

Trained for Empathy. Our security team is trained for empathy. They diffuse situations with care. Their goal is to keep the community safe without exerting unnecessary bouts of power. They are of service to the community and highly touted as patient, caring, and professional.

HAVING FUN

A Day Adventure

Shopping. For non-residents and residents alike, the shopping experience in The Neighborhood is stellar. With fashion from resident designers manufactured in The Neighborhood using homegrown fabric, we offer styles and quality you cannot get anywhere else. A variety of shops offer a range of products. Fragrances, toys, pottery, home decor, electronics, and more. All of which are made in The Neighborhood using resources grown in The Neighborhood.

Eating Out. Restaurants offer different cuisines and styles to enjoy. From traditional sit-down restaurants to restaurants that cater to a child's innate need to play. There are plenty of diverse ways to enjoy food in The Neighborhood.

Hair Cut Nails Did. The salon offers services to make everyone look and feel good. Everyone is catered to in a space designed to offer hair styling, manicures, pedicures, line ups, shaves, waxing, and makeup.

Physical Activity. A gym complex featuring rock climbing, weight lifting, basketball courts, racquetball, tennis, an Olympic-size pool with diving, and a track. Enjoy The Neighborhood skating rink or bowling alley for physical fun with a cocktail.

An Epic Night Out

Nightlife. Nightclubs host local DJs and offer a stylish atmosphere to drink, dance, and mingle. The dive bar is a low-key place to hang out and watch sporting events. The lounge is a nice in-between space that is comfortable meets chill.

Sporting Events. The Neighborhood hosts its own sporting club league featuring most mainstream sports. The gym complex hosts games with standard concessions and drinks available for patrons.

Museum. Local art is featured throughout The Neighborhood. A hub for art sales is the museum. The museum is a great place for local artists and art lovers to commune and host events.

Theatre. The theatre triples as a movie theatre, concert hall, and play venue. Along with cutting-edge performances put on by local talent, the movie theatre shows local films and mainstream blockbusters alike.

Our Network

The Neighborhood produces media content. We create news broadcasts, talk shows, reality tv, comedy series, drama series, game shows, music videos, movies, and documentaries. All content is hosted on our streaming service which is also translated into a channel for local television. Mainstream cable and streaming services such as Netflix, Amazon Prime, Hulu, Disney+ and insert your choice here, are all available to residents.

Never Forfeit Your Passion

In The Neighborhood, no resident has to give up their passion to pay the bills. Whether it's sports or the arts, every resident is encouraged to continue exploring their passion for as long or as little as they wish.

Travel

Residents can enjoy a staycation in the local resort or use their own money to travel the world. If they do not have enough funds to travel outside The Neighborhood, they can join a group vacation funded by The Neighborhood bank.

$$$

Every service offered to residents is available to non-residents for a price.

PART IV

THE NEXT STEPS

PATHWAY TO REALITY

This book is the first step in the plan to build The Neighborhood. Collaboration is the key to completion. Our pathway to reality begins with connecting people who have a passion for change.

The Greenprint Connection

Diverse sustainable environments must be designed in collaboration with those they serve. Our connection workshops foster collaboration built on dignity to ensure the best ideas come to fruition. The Greenprint holds Connection to nurture a relationship with the community, learn skills for compassionate collaboration, and carve out a space where we can imagine a better future. Skills we touch on are non-violent communication, diversity, equity, inclusion, sustainability, collaboration, and innovation. Our workshops are customized to our audience as we hold space for community and business. When a business purchases a workshop we match a workshop for another non-profit. Relationships and resources gained with this work help power our journey.

The Greenprint Virtual Reality

As we build community in Connection, we are simultaneously developing our VR design tool. Our virtual tool connects a global audience to design, build, and test our future neighborhood. The goal is to make the VR usable on any piece of prospective land. Our first venture is to design our pilot neighborhood. A community we build in the virtual to make a reality.

In the VR you can:
* *Walk around a 3D scan of the land*
* *Learn the land's history*
* *Build on the site by placing blocks that represent homes, gardens, farms, energy sources, and more*

❖ Ask and answer questions about the site
❖ Simulate population needs, resources, and financial management
❖ Explore the curated global build where you can connect with users
❖ As the design goes from macro to micro, The Greenprint provides
a detailed blueprint for building the community in the real world

Blueprint to Build

Using the blueprint created in the VR, we begin to build our first pilot neighborhood. Heads of departments take lead on construction carried out with contractors. A temporary campus was built on-site for heads to reside. They begin to hire and train residents in their prospective fields. As construction gets closer to completion, orientations for incoming residents take place.

Once construction is completed, the first group of essential leading residents moves in - 20% of the population. Our food, power, and water systems move into production. If they prove to be producing sustainably, the green light is given to move in more residents. This staggering rollout continues until all shops, restaurants, and amenities open.

We operate our pilot neighborhood for a minimum of two years before expanding. This time allows for feedback, adjustments, and upgrades. After proving successful, we use The Greenprint VR to develop the next prospective piece of land.

WAYS TO SUPPORT THIS JOURNEY

If you are inspired, here are some actions you can take to help The Neighborhood become a reality.

Share the Book

A solid supportive base can help this idea come to fruition. The easiest way to grow support is by sharing the book. Gift it, loan it, or share the link to the free download.

Host a Workshop

Connect with us in a workshop. Either join a community workshop we host or support by purchasing one for your organization. Every workshop purchased is matched with a free community workshop.

Expand the Network

Join our team of experts across fields to further the vision of The Neighborhood. Our departments include:

Agriculture	Culinary
Energy	Resource Management
Architecture	Communication
Construction	Technology
Education	Urban Planning
Healthcare	Marketing
Finance	Sanitation
Law & Security	Transportation

Donate

Since the first release of this book in January 2020, The Greenprint has grown into a 501c3 nonprofit organization dedicated to offering solutions to poverty, social injustice, and climate change by creating sustainable neighborhoods where a higher quality of life is accessible to all. All tax-deductible financial contributions go towards producing The Greenprint VR, buying the land, and procuring resources for building The Neighborhood.

Visit www.createthegreenprint.com to learn more.

Thank you for reading The Greenprint. With a vision, a plan, and a team of people who are brave enough to act, this seed can flourish. I am incredibly grateful for any eyes who grace these pages. Hopefully, you can join in the journey to forge an upgrade on life.

ABOUT THE AUTHOR

In January 2020, Jordyn Barber wrote a book titled The Greenprint, her call to reimagine cities and communities to address racial injustice, wealth inequality, and climate change without waiting for a financial or societal green light. It is a hope for future cities that represent all people in America to be created.

Having her MFA in Film & TV Production and BA in Interactive Media from the University of Southern California, she follows the mantra "the film is made in preproduction" and wholeheartedly believes creating an immersive plan for an ideal society is the most pragmatic way to see it manifest in reality.

She was born in Georgetown, South Carolina, a small town drenched in the history we would like to forget but must reconcile. This history propels her understanding that creating a culture that values dignity, sustainability, and innovation is the most pragmatic way for said society to last.